Walking in our Schoenen

By Heidi L. Arnold

As told by George Christian Bruggeman

Copyright © 2018 Heidi L. Arnold

All rights reserved.

ISBN: 978-1729733561

ISBN-13: 978-1729733561

DEDICATION

Lopin in our Schoenen is dedicated to our children—the legacy of the Bruggeman family. May you understand the importance of knowing where you've come from and how your ancestors arrived to this country. May you and the generations after us preserve the heritage that those before us worked hard to sustain including loving all humans no matter the color or nationality.

—Mom and Pop

CONTENTS

Acknowledgments	i
Then God	3
Where in the World	5
A History Lesson	15
God Became Real	16
Captive and Working	24
A Day to Remember	31
The Long Road Home	33
Shenanigans	40
God Showed Up	45
The Change	58
America	64
The Family	72
Ancestry	77
For the Future Generations	80
With an End, a Beginning	83

ACKNOWLEDGMENTS

As the writer of the story, I'd like to thank George and Jans for willingly sharing their family heritage with me. The time spent together has enriched my life.
Thank you to the Bruggeman children for allowing me to peek into your family stories and photos through the tales your parents told that are a part of your childhood.
Special thanks to my proofreader, Millie Hunsaker, for her tireless editing and knowledge.

THEN GOD

A young man of only 18 cried out, "God, help me!" as he intentionally jumped from his military motorbike to avoid a spray of bullets that he couldn't hear but could clearly see dimpling the dirt in front of him. A messenger for the Indonesian army serving on the island of Celebes, George was delivering information to Captain Wash when he saw a motion from the captain who was aiming his gun into the air. George saw a Zero, a Japanese war plane, with a red ball on the wings diving in his direction and knew he must abandon the moving bike. Using his best instinct and the guidance of the God's Holy Spirit, George jumped into a ditch hoping the Japanese would believe he were dead. And it worked; he left this incident unscathed, not even a scratch.

On another island more than 1,000 miles to the west was a petite girl of 11 riding her bicycle to the local waarzegster (tarot card reader) at her mother's request. Jans (YONCE), the oldest child, had been sent to ask a lady who read the cards if her father, who had been drafted into the war, was still alive. Her mom had sent her with money as she had many times before. The card reader's answer was always the same, "Your father is still alive!" Even at a young age, Jans knew it was a waste of her mother's money and disliked the visit. She was especially eager to leave during the times she encountered people of different religions whose appearance and behaviors scared her.

Only God could foresee that these two young people marry and conquer a life full of challenges. George was fighting for his own survival and for the freedom of his country which his family raised him to love. And Jans was learning responsibility by caring for her younger siblings and at the same time gaining an understanding of the harsh realities of life. The world war set the tone for each of their personalities, even before they met. Both had been born in Indonesia but were considered Dutch. People living in Indonesia at the time were either born Indonesian or born of Dutch decent. Without any reservations, George and Jans lived their lives as fully Dutch. Because of their commitment to their heritage, they were pressed to work hard and love hard to be the individuals they sought to be. To retain their Dutch nationality, they continually pushed against conformity and lived with a thread of negative nationalism that the world had sewn into their skin.

The following pages highlight their life story as told by each of them and depict a fight against their home country's independence which forced them to leave the land in which they were born. Their journey to Holland to embrace their Dutch heritage was a bitter pill, where racism showed itself, and the two felt discarded and abandoned by the only culture they knew. Taking another step into the unfamiliar land of the United States led to more adventures that heightened their determined strength and resolve to be a successful and productive family while clinging to the Dutch legacy they were given at birth.

WHERE IN THE WORLD

George and Jans were born in what is now called Indonesia. He was born on the island of Celebes or what we now know as the island of Sulawesi, and she was born on the main island of Java. Indonesia is comprised of almost 1,000 inhabited islands as well as hundreds of others that are uninhabited. The main islands (see below) are Java, Sumatra, Borneo, Bali, and

Sulawesi or Celebes where the most common language is Malay,) although nearly 300 dialects are spoken across the islands. These islands have more active volcanoes than any other country and contain six

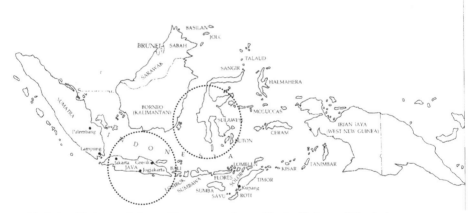

official religions: Islam, Protestantism, Catholicism, Hinduism, Buddhism and Confucianism.

George Christian Bruggeman was born on April 23, 1923 in the city of Macassar, located on the tip of the southern peninsula, of the island of Celebes. The island named by the Portuguese was later re-named Sulawesi after gaining independence from the Dutch. George was the first child born to Albert Hendrick and Emily Constantine Bruggeman who eventually had three more boys and three girls: Erna, Jenny, Loes, Edward, Albert Johann/Joe, and Rudy. Each called George by the name of Christian (CHRIS-TEE-AHN), Chris for short. When he immigrated to the United States, his co-workers called him George and it took him some time to determine for whom they were asking. (Albert Bruggeman, father, with his four sons: left to right, Eddie, Rudy, Joe, and George

Like the American Indian, Sacagawea, who helped explorers navigate their way to the American west in the early 1800's, George was talented with languages. Although his family spoke Dutch in the home, he learned several languages in the Dutch Indonesian School when he

was a boy. He also learned the languages spoken by the servants in their home who came from different places in the islands. In addition, George began mastering languages from all over while traveling with his dad when he had the opportunity. In the small villages, the natives needed money to start businesses. Since George's father worked for a bank that loaned money for these small businesses, George sometimes traveled with his dad to these small villages. These trips took place following harvest time when money was more readily available to re-pay the loans. As father and son traveled, George was exposed to various languages, enabling him to expand his language skills. By picking up these local languages, George was no longer restricted to knowing just Dutch and Malaya, the common, shared language of the country. He also learned a bit of English his senior year of high school. Because of his dad's business and record keeping, George was also good with money. "If there was a difference between two or three pennies, my dad would challenge me to find the mistake," he said.

Life before World War II was very easy, according to George. His family had customary servants living in a house behind the family home. George made it very clear that these people were an extension of their own family. His grandmother treated the servants like they were her own children. The servants' children were born and raised in the family and sometimes married into the family. Each servant had a specific responsibility; one was designated for the house cleaning, another for the washing, one for the cooking and one to walk George and his siblings to school. George said these families and their children all grew up with him and his siblings.

Wanting the best for their children and because of their own love for dancing, George's parents enrolled him in a dance school when he was 11 years old. "It was not boogie woogie but regular dance, like formal dance," George said. "That's where I learned, and I was pretty good!" One of the most important gifts from his parents was a gun. His father gave his mother a gun, but when George was 10 years old, she gave the gun to her son; hunting would become his favorite hobby. Like most kids around the world, kids living in Indonesia played soccer. George was no exception, using a soccer ball fashioned from pliable rattan. He lived a privileged life in Celebes—educated and loved and given ample experiences as he was growing up.

It was a child's dream to have mangoes growing right

outside the window of the house. George described the home as having living space upstairs, while the car was parked underneath the house. Varying fruit trees surrounded the house: lemon, papaya, and coconut. Mourning doves gathered in the nearby rice fields, so George was quick to kill them for eating. They fried doves and pigeons as well as ducks. "It was normal to shoot them from inside the window and then run outside and get them," he said. Coconuts were dried and grated and then cooked to retain the coconut oil to make soap.

While attending high school, George and all the boys participated in an ROTC-like training, practicing marching and falling down on a mat. As an adult, George now realizes that the training was mandatory because the government suspected a war could break out any time. As slight as it was, the training was all the boys had before going to war in 1941. Looking back, George realized that he didn't really think about his future or have much interest in what his life might hold before he was called to war.

> George said: "My father did have a coconut plantation and rice fields besides a fish farm in addition to his job. I've outlived my dad by 20

years, and I still remember one thing from when I was two or three years old. Every day I was standing in front of the house with my mom and when Dad came back from work, the first thing my dad did was pick me up and hug me so hard. I can never forget it as old as I am now. I can never forget it. I loved my dad."

When George was a young boy, the people in the villages knew his family well, and he was well respected by the community. He was an avid hunter and people were happy to allow him to hunt on their property. While hunting, young kids and parents would go outside carrying bamboo tong tongs (a homemade instrument that when hit on the outside produced a sound) to drive the wild boar and deer out. At the sound of tong, tong, tong, the animals would go running and the trained dogs would chase the animals out of the forest. George was grateful the only expense to him for hunting was giving the land owners some cigarettes in exchange for the chance to hunt. He explained property owners welcomed the hunters because the animals ruined the rice fields and sugar and potato plantations, so hunting helped to get rid of the varmints. Sometimes George would shoot a pellet gun from the window inside his home to kill a dove or two. "You shoot a few of them and have the servants prepare them. Whatever fell from the trees was fair for anyone to eat like coconuts or other fruits."

While seven-year-old George danced and played with his siblings, a little girl named Jans Sophie was born in Semarang on the island of Java on May 16, 1930. She lived with her mom and dad and eventually her two younger brothers and two sisters. Jans still dreams at night about the place—the trees and big buildings. Jans has no photographs because her life was surrounded by so much turmoil and unable to carry them with her. Her father, Fritz Rohder, a German man, was a bookkeeper who brought money home at night and had the responsibility of taking it to the bank in the morning. Her mother was Pauline Rohder of Dutch descent. Jans easily cried while talking about her mom and siblings; she said she matured quickly learning to care for her siblings, washing their clothes and making their food. At the same time that George and all men between 18 and 40 were called to war, Jans' father was drafted as well. When Fritz was killed during the war at 36 years old, Jans was only 11. "I believed all the time that he was alive," Jans said. "I went to the Red Cross every day with my bike to ask."

Jans felt all alone after her father had gone to war.

Jans' bike had hard, rubber tires, and she would be given a bag and sent out to get some groceries. Jans told the story of her mother's bag of jewelry containing a thick, golden bracelet that was a gift from her father. Jans believed her father understood he may never return from the war because he bought the bracelet. After the news of his death in a prison camp, Jans was required to take the bracelet to the Chinese store and ask them to cut a piece off the bracelet in exchange for money. This is how the family survived, she told. "Every time she said to me, 'Meid, can you go to the Chinese store," Jans knew exactly what she was to do and she'd hop on her bicycle to sell part of the only possession her father had left behind. "And so we lived for years on that bracelet," she said. She wonders even today why she had to be the oldest, taking on the responsibility of caring for her siblings in addition to having to endorse the loss of her beloved father. Little did she know how important maturing in this way would impact her life in the very near future.

After World War II began in 1941, the Indonesian

government moved the women and children to Thailand to protect them from the Japanese. Communism had started and Jans' mother, Pauline, packed a few valuables and the children and boarded a freight ship for a refugee camp. Still not knowing whether her husband Fritz was alive, she fled to Thailand for safety for her and the young children. Jans remembered learning life lessons from the people in that camp. "Sometimes you have a pillow, and sometimes you wouldn't," she said. "You'd have to lay down in the floor next to strange people." After the war ended, while they were still in Thailand the family received the news that Fritz, Jans' father, had died in a prisoner of war camp—probably months before they were given the news. Jans said her mother was just not herself after hearing the news. Later, they were moved to another refugee camp in Celebes.

A HISTORY LESSON

Portuguese sailors were the first to arrive in Indonesia in the 1500's, but it didn't take long for the Dutch—from what we know today as the Netherlands—to come seeking something to bring them wealth. The islands provided an abundance of nutmeg, cubeb pepper, cloves and cinnamon. Over the centuries, Dutch explorers were most interested in making money via trades and eventually colonized the archipelago. After accumulating great riches, the Dutch government consolidated all the competitors into a corporation: The Dutch East India Company, known to the Dutch as VOC. This was one of the first multi-national corporations. It began in 1602 and established a trade interaction with India and other Southeast Asian countries. After the company dissolved in 1800, the area formerly known as the East Indies was under Dutch colonial control and therefore was referred to as the Dutch East Indies. The term *Indonesia* was used as well in the 1880's.

Fast forward a century, and history tells that the Japanese were in search of Dutch oil to support its war efforts. Quickly overwhelmed by the Japanese, the Royal Dutch East Indies Army surrendered in 1942. Thousands of people died due to diseases, living conditions, and murder in Indonesia while the Japanese Empire occupied the country from March of 1942 until 1945. After WWII and with the Japanese surrender in 1945, the Dutch colony began to crumble. Leadership was still seeking Indonesian independence. The East Indies nationalists wanted to remove the Dutch tie from their country since the Japanese had promised independence to them. From the first inception of independence, the people of Indonesia bickered about what the islands should be called and who was welcome there. In 1949, Indonesia finally gained independence from the Dutch.

GOD BECAME REAL

When Pearl Harbor was attacked on a Sunday morning in 1941, it was already lunchtime on Monday in Celebes. The Netherlands and Indonesia were allies with America, so the Dutch Queen from the Netherlands, Queen Wilhelmina, was the first to declare war on Japan. George said the men 18 years and older were told to report for duty the next day. They were given uniforms, guns and some drills to learn to shoot. The uniform was grayish green with gray leggings and combat boots. George described the Dutch helmets much like the American helmets of today. Only a month later, the men were fighting with only long rifles with bayonets against machine guns. The men fought the Japanese on their home territory, close to home from December until March.

After fighting the Japanese on their own soil and being captured and confined for seven months, the strong men were sent to Japan—almost a year after the war began.

> "When the troops started infiltrating, they came out from the river and through the cornfield. We used a firing arm to mow them down," George said. The ones that fell down, we just stepped over and keep on going. That was our first fight with them, only about 10 miles from the city. I am good in shooting because I am big hunter. I aimed at the head, shoulders, whatever was sticking out."

At first, George used his language skills to work with the coolies who were laborers speaking an Indonesian language. Eventually, George was given the responsibility to carry messages via motorbike from one command post to the next. Because there were no walkie-talkies, he relayed information face-to-face with written instructions about pulling back or whether to go east or west or reporting information regarding how far the enemy had advanced. George's use of languages enabled him to qualify for this position as well. In the beginning, fighting took place in the hills and jungles of Celebes, places the boys and men knew well. Maps were available but not really needed. George told of how they slept in the bush and endured hot temperatures during the day and night.

They used, ate, and drank whatever they could find available in the jungle. (George Bruggeman, who would become Corporal Bruggeman)

George said: "And wherever you can find some booze, you booze and booze and booze because you want to forget what is happening the next day. Am I still gonna be here or not? When you come together at night, all your buddies and schoolmates, you look and wonder: will I still be here tomorrow night? You don't know."

During the first week of the fighting, George was on the side of a hill looking down the side of another hill where a company was surrounded and being attacked by the Japanese. He remembered seeing a truck pass by a little later. His eyes struggled to realize the reality of what he saw: a pair of boots sticking out of the back. His attitude toward war changed on the next day when he found out the boots were on the feet of

his 38-year-old uncle, the younger brother of his father. He'd been hit by a mortar shell that split his head open. George was never the same after that. "When I heard this, it drove me crazy. The one thing on my mind was kill, kill, kill—whenever you can." George reminisced about how unreal it was to shoot a human. "After the first one, you have one thing in mind: kill or be killed." Knowing that his family and friends were being killed removed the feeling of being sorry and replaced it with a feeling of hate. All these years later, George thinks how senseless it was to kill—no need for any of it.

In the beginning, the men had to destroy their own country's gas stations and buildings so the Japanese couldn't use them. George said, "Everything they could use, we blew up before we pulled back into the hills and jungle and mountains." During the fighting, George focused on the caps of the soldiers; this is how he could discern between his own comrades and the Japanese. While on a mountain or hill looking down, the men would shoot caps. "You kill them or not; you don't know," George said. They didn't have any other strategy but to shoot and go onto the next one. Because the Indonesians were dressed in green uniforms, George and his comrades would see green and immediately know these were their buddies. While in the jungle, the men would shoot and run in between the rice and sugar cane fields. George said when he saw leaves moving, he just fired into them. Later, he would question why he did that knowing he could kill a person. However, he knew if he *didn't* kill, he would *be* killed. George said killing a person stayed with him for a very long time and left the question of why it had to be done and whether a man could be forgiven for doing it.

On occasion, the enemy stole clothes from the dead bodies to trick the Indonesian army. If a soldier believed a man in green was his ally and approached him, the fraud would open fire. George and his comrades had heard how brutal the Japanese could be if found by them. "I heard they cut the penis off of some of the men they killed. They cut the face or chest open while they are dead already," he said. If one of their own men were killed, they left them to rot. They could not stop or take time to bury them or carry them to safety. George recounted those long days and nights of thinking about getting out alive and seeing his family again. Every night he had one question in his mind: "Will I make it until tomorrow night?"

While in the field, the men were desperate for water. Like animals drinking in the forest, the soldiers would drink tiny puddles of rain water that collected in large jungle leaves. George believed the heat from the sun kept the bacteria at the bottom of the puddles, so he and his buddies sipped the top of the puddles. He remembered one time they came upon a little stream, and of course, everyone ran to get water. One of the lieutenants got up the nerve to tell people who did not belong to his particular company to wait their turn. George and his comrades were so mad that he said, "It wouldn't have been much of a problem to put a bullet in the lieutenant's head." The lack of water was so great that the men were angry and irrational.

These first few months tried George's patience and stamina and his faith in humankind. It was during this time that he personally encountered the God of the universe. As he spent much of his time on the road traveling from post to post delivering commands from one officer to another, he pondered the reasons for war and the purpose for living. One day, when the enemy spied him from the sky and tried to kill him as he rode on his motorbike, he called out to the God his parents had raised him to know. George asked God to help him, and He did. This was the first time George knew for certain that Jesus Christ was alive and in the business of saving people—physically, financially, spiritually, and emotionally. His personal journey with God began that day in the ditch with his chest heaving and his young mind spinning.

So, in May of 1942—after three months of hard fighting—the Japanese captured the Indonesian army after the army of Java had capitulated. The Japanese presented the army with an ultimatum. They commanded them to surrender or they would hurt the elderly, the women and the children who were living in refugee camps. Many families who owned plantations had also been forced to make room on their property for the elderly as well as women and children. George remembered how at that time he fought hard so that he could see his parents and siblings again. He and his comrades would not let them kill their families. So they surrendered. (Asama-Muru circa 1931 from Google images)

George and many others were housed in a camp, which was originally their own Indonesian camp. "Surrounding us with their soldiers, they lined us up and took us to the army camp we used to use," George said. In October of 1942, the Japanese began sorting the young, strong men from the weak and/or sick. The strong ones, which included George, were sent to Japan to work and live in a prisoner of war camp. They were boarded onto The *Asama Muru*, a transport boat which first launched in 1928 and sank in 1944 in the South China Sea. The boat also carried Aussies and Brits who had been shot down in planes by the Japanese.

CAPTIVE AND WORKING

On The *Asama Muru*, more than 1,000 soldiers were crammed into the hold for eight or nine days while en route to

Japan. "The hold was very crowded," George said. "We had to sit or lean back to sleep. We took turns and waited for each other to use the bathroom. If you could get a bucket, it would be best." The strong men spent the next three years on the northern shore of the island of Kyushu in a town called Fukuoka where the Japanese guarded them and ordered them to march and to work. Men from different countries including England, United States, and Australia were in the camp. George continued to use his language skills and was valuable to the men living near him, enabling them to communicate. The men worked six days a week, 12 hours a day for more than three years in a shipyard, building warships for Japan.

Even though they were not fed well, George said it was important to eat to have sufficient strength to not only work but to live. During work, prisoners were given a sardine can containing rice topped with a little piece of dried fish or dehydrated vegetable. After work, the same thing would be served for dinner.

> George said, "For breakfast we got a kind of soup that was like dishwater plus a little bowl of rice. At lunch we had a piece of dry corn or maybe a white carrot and a little rice. At night it was the same — soup with nothing in it and rice. Just enough to keep us alive. I started at 168 pounds and

then at the end of the war, I was bones in a bag. You could hardly see any meat—only bones."

It was even more critical for the men to eat if they were not feeling well. If a man did not have food in his system to fight a sickness, he would surely die.

> "They get sick, they throw up. They get sick, they throw up. They don't want to eat anymore", George said. "I had pneumonia two times in there. But whatever they give me to eat, no matter how bad I feel, how worse it is than the last time, I keep eating. Eat and throw up. Eat and throw up. That got me through all the pain and sickness, and I came out of it."

Of course, the clothing they wore became threadbare and with their stomachs empty, they were not only fighting the situation in their minds, but also in their stomachs and the battle of staying strong and warm. Compounding the situation was the fact that the Indonesian men were born in a tropical climate and were shipped to Japan with light clothing. When the first winter came, the men were each issued an old Army coat, but it was not heavy enough to combat the cold.

> "If we found a piece of paper or cardboard on the ground, we'd pick it up, hide it from the guards and then put it under our shirts as underwear to stay warm," George said.

"But you make sure they don't see it because they are going to beat you to death. You hide it under your clothing."

And once a week, they could take a sponge bath. Each man stood in a long line holding a sliver of soap and a towel while waiting his turn. Restroom use required another long line. Men would "go" in a stream of water that flowed into a big container. George delighted to tell how the Japanese used the contents of that container for their farms. The furnishings of the camp were sparse and included wooden bunks for each man which were enclosed in long buildings.

Everyone who encounters a trauma like war and imprisonment needs an outlet, a way to fight the system and fill the mind with hope in order to keep going. George found this will to survive by holding onto the dream of marrying a 17-year-old girl named Hendrika. The daughter of a bread baker, Rika, as she was called, met George before the war broke out. He proposed to her and promised he would return to marry her. While traveling on the nine-day boat trip to Japan, the men were in the hold of the ship passing the time by using Chinese ink to make tattoos on their bodies. It seemed only right that George have one on his arm to remind him of Rika. "I told her I would come back," he said. "I did promise to marry her. When I make a promise, I hate to break it. She kept me alive out there; I was grateful." The thought of Rika waiting for him allowed him to endure a few beatings and two bouts of pneumonia.

In addition to surviving the cold and the sickness and the lack of nourishment, George and the men suffered punishment from the guards.

> George said, "They beat people on their chests or backs with a long stick so bad they would bleed. If a person was caught smoking, the guards would force them to tell how they got the cigarette. Sometimes men would enter the restroom during our work time and the guys would say, 'Sshhhh, sshhhh' and offer half a stub of a cigarette to someone to finish. If they got caught, they get the beating of their life."

Another form of punishment involved inserting a rod behind the knees of the victim and forcing the person to sit. Still another form of brutality, employed when a soldier did not do what was requested, was to endure watching the enemy tie something heavy to the end of a piece of a three-foot long, boat rope knowing he would "hit the hell out of you," George explained. George suffered fewer beatings than most because he understood bits of Japanese. If a man had no understanding of what a guard was saying, then complying was even more difficult.

> George said, "I tried from the beginning to understand their language. If you understand their language, you know what they want. If you do not know what they want, they smack you right in your face. I had several slaps on my face, but was never punished with the rope. But I did sit on my butt with the stick behind my knee for about 30 minutes. It seems like a very long time."

Another reason for a beating was accepting food from the Japanese women in the shipyard who sometimes smuggled in a fruit or tomato for the prisoners. If caught, the guards would beat the man for accepting it and the woman for giving it. The guards "beat the hell out of the women like they would beat a man," he said. George realized that Japanese natives had feelings too, and amazingly after a few days, the women would start smuggling again. "They [the Japanese] were not all bad."

When the men arrived in Japan that fall, they were trained to rivet, drill, and plate in order to build ships. People from all nations learned and built: Koreans, Americans, British, even Japanese people. George helped create ten or 11 cargo ships during his time there. The days started before six o'clock in the morning with guards having the men form a line and then calling off their numbers. "Mine was 784," George easily recalled. Being told what to do and where to be every minute of the day was difficult, but being called by a number was demeaning. During a 15 minute-walk to the shipyard, many men had opportunity to plot some sort of sabotage. George said, "I remember one American named Matthew who was working in the riveting group. He hated it so much that one day he threw a rivet hammer on his foot just to get off work." The men also tried to sabotage the ship.

> George said, "You had to rivet straight and then the controller would come with a hammer and tap on the rivet to hear the sound. He could tell by the sound if it's okay or not. If you put the rivet in at an angle, it would cause movement and could cause the rivet to fall out and make the ship fall apart. And if you've done it incorrectly in several places on a plate, they consider that to be boycotting them. We also would make the boards loose so the guards would fall off of them. We tried to do what we can do to make life miserable for them."

To keep from becoming bored and to get some exercise when they were not working, the men spent time boxing with one another. George said, "The Japanese loved it, especially if someone was beat up. The Japanese would cheer for me if I beat someone up. I lost, and I won." Inside the camp, they heard no news. Once in a while, somebody would smuggle a piece of newspaper, but it was in Japanese, nothing in English or any other language they could read. They had no idea what was going on in the world. The Red Cross was faithful to send packages for the prisoners, but they rarely received any portion of them. The Japanese guards would enjoy the contents of the boxes and give one box to four or five prisoners to divide. Food-related problems frequently instigated fights. George told a story about a friend whose dad was in the prison camp. His food was stolen by a young, healthy guy. George said, "I was so mad. I beat the hell out of the guy. Why does he have to steal food from an older man? It's the only time I beat someone. They had to take me off of him, but he never stole again."

A DAY TO REMEMBER

One morning, August 9, 1945—almost three years after George had been taken captive—he and others were working on a ship with four decks, each with a ladder leading up to the next floor. They saw a flash, much like one they'd seen several times before. Once in a while, a flash was created by two pieces of sheet metal clashing together as they were lifted to an upper deck. When they saw that flash, they realized it was different somehow. At the same time, they felt a hot wind under the decks and heard a BOOM! The men feared a bomb might have landed on the ship. Mayhem ensued and men scattered for shelter. Then they saw a cloud of fire and smoke and heard the noise of planes. Not until later did they learn that the United States had just dropped an atomic bomb on Nagasaki, a mere 95 miles from their worksite. They heard later it killed 74,000 people and injured many more. The prisoners working on the ship were ushered into a shelter until that afternoon when it was clear what had happened. Before the day was over, a ferry boat came to the nearby island carrying injured people who had been burnt and were blackened. Before leaving work, George and his workmates were told there would be no work for three days and the next day would be devoted to prayer.

George said, "The Japanese commanders said today is a day to pray. We did not know they were capitulating. The second day we were all called into the camp and the English commander and the Japanese commander said, 'Well, we have decided to quit the war. Not to lose the war but to quit the war.' The Japanese guards turned in their guns, and that is how we know Japan lost the war."

Even though the war was over, the men did not leave the camp right away. During this time, George learned that his 23-year-old cousin, Albert, was sick and no medicines were available. "I visited Albert several times in the sick bay," George said. "But guys just gave up. He really was not a fighter and didn't have the will. He was too weak to keep on going." It wasn't until the day after George had seen Albert, the guards told him Albert had died. George was offered the privilege of escorting his cousin on the ferry boat from the camp to the place of cremation in Nagasaki. "It's just like when you bring someone you love to the graveyard here in the States." George said the trip was about 45 minutes and involved dropping off the bodies and returning to camp. He knew his cousin's body would be burned. The only honorable thing to do for his family was to go. "When I took my cousin to be buried, I saw the city [Nagasaki] completely flat down to the ocean, those iron posts and lamp posts all melted on the ground."

THE LONG ROAD HOME

After the liberation, George heard that many prisoners took their anger out on the Japanese guards. They wanted to give them beatings like they had endured. Some of them even killed the guards after the war was over. George went into a little village one day and saw the Japanese bow to greet Indonesian men with respect. He even saw a Japanese officer offer to give up his sword. This convinced George that the Japanese did not hate those who had been captured. After many weeks, the American ship, *Chenango,* came to Nagasaki. All the prisoners were rescued by patrol torpedo boats and taken to the ship. George said it was then that better food came their way.

> George said, "The first food we ate was like going to heaven. They slaughtered some pigs, so we had good food. It is a feeling I'll never forget after all the misery for three and a half years. We come on the ship, the deck comes up, a breakfast on the deck and they play beautiful music. We do not know what comes over us. And the first meal we were served was like we were in paradise."

After another trip, they were taken to Okinawa and finally the men were taken to Manila, Philippines for a few months while waiting for transportation back to Indonesia. George loved the American music that was provided for them and enjoyed the WAC girls. "The Women's Army Corps brought women to entertain us at the canteen. That's where I learned to do the Jitterbug. So when I went back to Indonesia, everybody wanted to learn from me," he said.

Finally by 1946, George and others, including Australian troops, were delivered to a camp in Macassar on his home island, where there was an airfield. His family and friends were there to welcome him home and to see who had survived the war. He expected Rika to be waiting. He did not see her and wondered where she could be. Eventually, his buddies came aboard the ship and broke the news that Rika had married while he was gone. He was very upset but later realized she had saved his life. The thought of returning home to Rika kept him hoping and striving to survive. Without his commitment to return home to Rika, George may have given up. He also came to understand how marriage protected Rika during a time when single women were in jeopardy of prostitution and other mistreatment by the Japanese. "I'm glad she didn't come back. Jans is the lucky one!" George said. The homemade tattoo of a heart and cross with Rika's name printed over it has reminded him throughout his life how God protects and brings hope even during dreadful situations.

Although George was brokenhearted, he had no idea the one who would be the love of his life was so very close there in the Macassar refugee camp. Jans, then around 16 years old, and her family had been brought to Macassar as well after living for months in Bangkok in a camp with other women and children. By this time, Jans knew her father had died and was still longing for her home in Java where she had spent years that were quiet and not so miserable. Thousands of women and children had been brought to the camp for protection, and Jans remembered how crowded it became after the men returned. The Red Cross provided supplies for everyone there. Jans said, "They gave us everything: food, clothing, supplies, and blankets. We had nothing left from our home. All of our belongings were gone, and the Red Cross was the only one who help us."

The men, including George, were so happy to be home. He said he hardly recognized his father when he came home because his hair was gray. Even though Rika had not shown up to greet him, he was excited just to see women again and to see his own family. It wasn't long before George was asked to form a band with some of his military buddies so they could entertain the troops. "We had a piano, trumpet, saxophone, clarinet, bass, drums and I played guitar. I was a crooner!" George worked to keep people on the dance floor and taught the girls the Jitterbug and other dances he had learned in Manila. Their ensemble, called *The Welfare Band,* played dances and appeared live on the radio twice a month. The band traveled some and it wasn't long before George fell in love with a woman, Karla, with a beautiful voice who also played the guitar. He kept a long-distance relationship with Karla until during one show George spotted a pretty teenage girl dancing and asked a bandmate, "Who's that?" The man who played in the band knew the girl because she was his niece. It didn't take long for George to find a way to dance with the young beauty: Jans

Sophie Rohder. Because George was so enchanted with Jans, he quickly said goodbye to his girlfriend Karla so he could fully pursue Jans.

Even though the war was over and the celebration of life was in full swing for George and Jans, serious changes were happening in Indonesia. The Communist Party of Indonesia was moving forward on the island of Java.

(George dancing with his oldest daughter, Edith)

Gullible young men were handed guns and given training, a macho thing for young boys. Sukarno was the first president of Indonesia and was leading the fight for independence from the Netherlands. Communism is what propelled the boycott of whatever was Dutch. If Dutch people were not willing to change their nationality to Indonesian, then others would make life miserable for the Dutch. The Netherlands' queen was pro-Dutch, but there was fighting in the streets against the communist people. George said, "If the communists killed somebody because of the fight for independence, they swiped blood from the corpse onto their finger and licked it! Communism had started, and this is what happened after the war."

Just like in the war, people identified their friends with a green hat.

> "We would greet men on the street by saying, 'Haba haba joe!' [How are you doing, Friend?]. We knew he was a friend of our country," George said. But the communists knew this saying and began speaking to us on the street with "Haba haba joe." And if we spoke back to him, he might kill you instead of saying hello."

The Indonesian people were unhappy and mean since they were fighting a war within the country after the long battle of World War II. It was only now that George realized the mandatory ROTC training he had in high school had only been mandatory for the Dutch boys, not for the Indonesian boys, even though Dutch nationals and native Indonesians were amicable before the war. The Dutch people were living in fear of being killed in their own villages. George told of one instance when he and his cousin returned from the grocery store and the women of the house asked why they their clothes were so dirty. They said how they had rushed from ditch to ditch on the way home in order to avoid being shot.

Jans also remembered a terrifying event regarding the Communists when she was a young girl. She said, "Red and Whites climbed up a banana tree outside my aunt's window and shot like the wild, wild West!" Her aunt had been shot in the side of her breast and moaned and cried out in pain. Jans watched as her aunt squeezed the bullet out from her skin and ripped down the mosquito netting from over the bed and wrapped herself in it to stop the bleeding. "It was nothing for them to take what they wanted like a sewing machine," she said. "They took the prized possessions of people who had nothing." It was after a similar raid that Jans remembered her aunt said to gather her clothes because they were leaving the next morning for Bangkok.

Everything suffered during this time. Before the war, the country still used the Dutch guilder, silver coins and paper money. Guilders devalued when the Japanese were in the country after the war. George described a day when the money had to literally be cut in half. A five dollar bill was only worth $2.50 and the people cut the paper. After the country gained independence, the value of the guilder went down even more. In dollars, two guilders was about the same value as one American dollar before the country began using rupiahs.

SHENANIGANS

As the country was changing, true love developed between Jans and George. Jans was certain George was the man of her dreams; however, her mother was not happy to hear about George because, at the time, Jans was engaged to a boy named Theo whom she had met in Bangkok. Theo taught Jans how to dance and would provide a good home for her. Jans said, "He gave me everything. One day I came home, and my whole bed was full with Max Factor make up!" Her mother was impressed with this gesture of wealth. Then one day when Jans was in the yard of her family home swinging in a big tree, George arrived. Her mother asked what he was doing there and Jans simply said she was going to go out with him for New Year's Eve. Her mother reminded her Theo was coming, and Jans assured her that he was not. She forbade Jans to go to the party with George, so Jans simply gained her mother's permission to go to the party with a nephew instead. What her mother didn't know was that Jans planned to meet George at the party! George said, "I was dancing with her again and this time I said, 'Hey, I'm gonna kiss you!' And then I did, right in the middle of the dance floor." Jans remembered the story the same way. She then described him as good looking. "He just had a way about him," she said. George offered Jans all he had in his pocket—chocolate from the army supply. "George gave me a bar of chocolate, and I fell for it!" Jans said.

Eventually, Jans wrote Theo a letter to break off the engagement. Her mother insisted on delivering the letter herself. But George was wise to his future mother-in-law's intentions. He posted the letter himself to ensure its safe arrival in Theo's hands. And it didn't take long for George to win over his mother-in-law's heart through his teasing and his genuine love. Even after George and Jans married, Theo visited Jans and asked if she was really happy. And of course, she was.

During these times, young people danced and socialized for fun. The young men would lift all the ladies into the back of a truck and go out together. Jans said, "The boys never thought about sex. No! They only wanted fun—dancing and singing. Sex was not included. We went with the group often and had a lot of fun. Guys had respect for girls back then." Big parties were fun for them even if their parents were unsure about the event. The young people found a way to attend even if it meant sneaking out of the house or climbing over a fence. "We loved big parties! We were wild!" Jans said with her trademark laugh.

George was very protective of Jans because he was concerned that other soldiers might see Jans and pry her away from him. Although he was devoted to only Jans, she told how he flirted with everybody for fun. George and Jans made a commitment to marry, but their families were steeped in different faiths. The challenges of marrying outside of the family's faith were great and some believed them to be insurmountable. (George and Jans' wedding day)

Jans was raised Catholic, so permission from the Pope was needed to marry a Protestant like George. Jans said, "I waited for a letter from the Vatican for a few months to get permission." After receiving a letter of permission from the Pope, wedding plans were made. George was invited to go hunting that day with his friends, but he reminded them he had a wedding to attend that morning! So on May 6, 1947, Jans and George married—twice. The first ceremony was in the Catholic chapel and the second was immediately after in the Protestant church with all in attendance at both ceremonies.

Just 10 days before Jans turned 17, she changed the course of her life by marrying George. "He was a son of a gun, and I loved him," Jans said. The newly married couple, their families and friends began celebrating. George's friends delivered their hunting bounty to the small celebration house where happy people filled the yard. Jans was a bit uneasy about the responsibility of feeding all the people, but her new mother-in-law was known for her cooking and told Jans to not worry. Emily Bruggeman said, "Everybody has to eat!" The celebration continued until around four o'clock in the morning.

GOD SHOWED UP

Because George was the head of the military warehouse, he was asked to remain in the military until 1947. His assignment was to drive a supply truck to the military posts around the island to deliver items like soap and shaving cream to the soldiers of Celebes. He and Jans traveled the roads together staying in villages, meeting people, and providing necessities. (George third from the left in front of the military supply van)

During a vacation to Java, George and Jans went dancing with

George's sister in tow. His sister told the band her brother was a good singer and they should let him sing. Before the end of the night, they offered him a job, but he just laughed at them. George stayed in the military as a civilian worker and eventually trained the lieutenant to take his place in the warehouse. Because of her experience caring for her siblings, Jans found married life a natural fit for her. Because she was living away from her own mother, Jans learned to really cook from Emily, her mother-in-law, by carefully observing. According to Jans, George's mother had secret recipes.

One recipe for a very ornate cake with layers, was only shared with Jans. She promised to never share it. "I love her dearly. Sometimes I love her more than my own mom", Jans said. "She teach me everything." Within a year, she was pregnant with their first child. When the baby arrived, George was excited to be a father and happy to have a wife who could so capably care for his children. (George singing as a guest)

Life in the Bruggeman household was never dull. At one point, George and Jans took in a monkey as a family pet. The monkey was ruining the floors by digging up plants in the neighbor's yard and dragging dirt through the house. Jans said, "I was so mad one day that I shot him with a BB gun. He was all of a sudden gone, and I said, 'Good!' The neighbors were mad at me for chasing off the monkey, but the floors were nice again."

(George, second from left, hunting boar with friends)

George also decided the family should have a pet bird, so he went to the forest and found a gorgeous green and yellow cockatoo. He brought it home to live in the front yard with a long chain hooked around its leg. Of course, they had dogs too. One memorable event was when one of their dogs bit their oldest son—leaving a lifetime scar on his cheek. And when George went hunting for wild boar and deer, the neighbors' dogs "chased little piggies out of the woods," George said. He kept the piglets, of course, to raise for food.

But pets and piglets weren't the only animals involved in the life of the Bruggemans. George continued to hunt and fish, as he had as a young boy, and even taught Jans how to clean the guns and cook the meat. Jans said, "He went fishing every weekend, and I stayed home to care for the children." During one hunting trip, George spied two boars sleeping in the woods. He was focused on killing at least one of the boars and didn't realize that a boa constrictor was curled up sleeping next to the boar! Startled at first, but energized in the next moment, he killed both the snake and the boar. He and his friends carried them out of the woods, sold the skins, and ate the meat. Jans would cook almost any game, but not snake. "I won't have anything to do with it," she said. "I was stupid enough to cook any of it in the first place…and to keep doing it."

Another time George was alone hunting alligator near a river. He walked along the bank and spied an alligator sunning itself and believed he could get close enough to shoot it. However, before he could get there, he stepped in quicksand. He tried to leverage his gun to get out of the hole but nothing worked. He quickly sank! He cried out to God for help, just like he had done the day the Japanese were shooting at him from the sky. And as he had hoped, God sent help. A native villager who had been in the woods nearby collecting firewood saw George. "He came running to me, and he get me out of it. He spread the wood out and pulled me out. I know God is always with me," he said.

George and Jans never met a stranger; they were always friendly and welcomed many people over the years to sit at their table for a meal or conversation. George worked with people of all nationalities during his life. He told of an ambassador to France who became a fishing buddy and family friend: "We always laughed so hard at our friend Vic. We were on an airplane headed to Java for a business trip, and Vic and others realized he smelled horrible and right there on the plane, he remembered he had previously fished in the shirt he was wearing—and the breast pocket was filled with rotten shrimp!"

Through a hunting venture, George and Jans met a Texan businessman and sporting store owner named Arlis Minter who came to Celebes to help build a cement factory. George had been hunting wild boar and was driving home with one on top of his jeep when Minter saw it. A friendship began, and Minter discerned that George was a hard worker and might be interested in moving from Indonesia one day. He offered to sponsor the family to come to Texas if they ever decided to immigrate.

In any spare time, George hunted for wild boar and alligators and a variety of other animals. He hunted ban tangs with antlers, wild boar, deer, panther, buffalos, jaguars, alligator—everything. When Jans was two months pregnant with our second daughter, I took her alligator hunting with me," George said. "We hunted them at night in a row boat with a flashlight."

(George, middle, with friends and a captured alligator)

He used a flashlight to see the blinking eyes of a gator as he navigated the river. He got as close as he could because, if not, the gator would sink down and the current of the river underneath would take it away.

> "You have to be close enough to get them in the boat," George said. "You shoot, grab its leg, and pull it in the boat. I eat the meat and sell the skin at the Chinese store, and they make things of it. My father and other elders always told me you shoot to kill. Don't do it just to waste. So I eat panther, snake, alligator, and wild boar. I have to try it! You don't waste life! This is one thing my dad teach me. If you want to eat it, you kill it. You don't do it just for the fun of it. My wife learned a lot. I teach her to skin a boar and clean my guns."

Jans interrupted his story with a shrill laugh. "He is too lazy to do that!"

"I am <u>tired</u>, not lazy," he said with a smile.

After leaving the military, George was in the business of importing and exporting, and many of his clients were Chinese. George said if he showed up at the Chinese store at 8 or 8:30 a.m., the very first thing they wanted him to do was sit down and have a drink of whiskey! The Chinese owners thought they were wise to get men to drink and not think straight. George said the plan of the businessmen was to acquire all of the good products—called 'ham stuff'—so the Chinese could make the most money with the best products. But George was astute. He knew better and was interested in dividing the best goods among all of his customers.

George believed he prospered because of his fair business practices. If a businessman was struggling to sell something, George did the best he could to help him. Beyond his pay from his work, George made money by helping people to sell their products.  (George with colleagues)

He also taught dancing lessons. "We always like to go to the parties and to have parties," George said. If the Bruggemans threw a child's birthday party, the Chinese would want to be there to participate and learn to dance. George laughed just thinking about how hard it was to teach them to dance. "They can't keep the beat! My sister and Jans and her sister all assisted me. We had a good time."

The Bruggeman family property in Celebes housed a coconut plantation and fish farm located between the ocean and the rice fields. The family lived in a brick house which had three bedrooms and three rooms in the back for the servants. Servants were like family in that era and stayed in the house of the family for which they worked. George and Jans had one to cook; one to do laundry; one to do cleaning; and one to help the kids. They would walk them to school in the morning. It was common for Dutch families to have nice homes; whereas, the Indonesian people lived mostly in bamboo houses. Since George's grandfather was "married" to the princess, they lived nicely. "It's normal for families to have help. We each made our own food, but we always ate together. At the back of the house was a pavilion which was built onto the main house. This was like a closed-in porch and was where George spent his time.

But their property was not the only place to find abundant food. According to George and Jans, Indonesia was lush with fruits and plenty of food to eat. Jans said she had such fond memories of going to the mountain to see George's aunt whose property was full of blooming trees in the spring. She described the women in the mountains who carried baskets of durian on their heads. (Durian is a thorny covered fruit with an unpleasant odor that Indonesians either love or hate.) "It is the best fruit—so sweet, and I will never forget those times." Jans said her mouth began to water just thinking about eating a durian. George laughed at the memory. He recalled how his wife enjoyed visiting the relatives but was anxious to get back home to her regular routine. The two looked at each other and laughed. "There goes the pepper tree!" George shouted! "When you eat a hot pepper and they make you dance, that is what she looked like when she was ready to go!"

One of the country's significant cultural aspects involved spirituality. George's mother, Emily, was a Christian who believed in God and had been trained to help those who had a spirit come into their body. Mysticism is strong in Indonesia, so her husband believed she was being helpful and supported her decision to help people in this way. However, Emily's husband left the spirit business to his wife. "He doesn't mangle with it," Jans said. Emily was known to heal people with prayers and holy water. She had the gift of prophecy—the ability to see things happening. George told how one of the kings in Java was a very good friend with his grandfather. When the king died, his gold belt was given to George's grandfather, and it was passed on to Emily as her inheritance. This belt was the tool that caused Emily to become involved in healing people. The belt housed the spices and herbs used to fight spiritual possessions within a person.

(Albert and Emily Bruggeman)

One time Emily was called to assist a healer from the island of Ambon. His name was Ambus, and he taught George how to do the process and to burn the incense. "If she cannot get a hold of Ambus, I help my mom," George said. Emily received the belt from her mother and kept it in a bag. Before Emily left Indonesia for Holland, she gave it to her sister who remained in Indonesia. "Nobody knew what was really in the bag," Jans said. "And nobody was allowed to touch it. It stayed in the bag and it doesn't get used up." George described the process like this:

> "Sometimes if somebody get killed at a specific place and another person disrespect it, the spirit get into you. The soul of the person get into you, and it start to talk to you. There was a field where a woman had been killed by the Japanese. A Chinese neighbor behind us had horses, and a guy bring the horses to an open field to graze every day. One day he came back from the field and *plop*; he fell down and was stiff like he was out. They called the doctor to check him out and can't find anything wrong. I look at him and I knew what was happening. A Catholic priest was there and he prayed and prayed. They all stood there and didn't know what to do. Jans was there and gave me a piece of pepper. And I finally hit the spot, and he started to talk. But this time the voice was a woman. People think I am crazy, but when you've been through it, you believe."

When the peppercorn was rubbed on the arm in just the right spot, the spirit would yell, "Let me go! Let me go!" Then George asked, 'Who are you? And why are you doing this?' The spirit spoke in her native language and told George she was punishing the person because 'he dirtied my house.' The spirit explained that the horses pee'd and pooped on that space where she died. She could no longer keep herself clean anymore and wanted to punish him for it. George told the spirit that he would bring flowers and burn some Indonesian spices. He asked the spirit to let the man go and assured her that the horses would no longer come there. Minutes later, the affected man opened his eyes and asked for a glass of water.

It is a bit dangerous to do this kind of work because the ghosts can rub off onto the person trying to help. Jans remembered a day it happened to her mother-in-law: "One day I saw her like a devil. She is possessed. It is the kind of thing you see in the movies." One incident resulted in the spirit telling George that everything will be all right when he goes overseas. This was years before he considered moving to the Netherlands, so he was mystified about the message. Another time, Jans' sister was sick and the doctor had no cure. They realized they would need to go to the ducan [the Dutch name for this kind of healer] because she had stepped on a grave and could not walk. The ability to utilize this gift left a rift between Emily and her son Eddie. He believed his mother was playing with the devil; however, when his daughter was very sick and near death, Emily healed her granddaughter with prayers and holy water. She waited patiently to be reunited with her son but died without ever seeing him again.

THE CHANGE

In 1949, Indonesia became independent; therefore, Dutch people were asked to change their nationality. Because of this, Dutch people began boycotting.

> "Things got very nasty on the street — all boom, boom, boom — and I had to sleep with two Colts 45's under my pillow," George said. "All the Dutch schools closed and the teachers went back to the Netherlands. We could have stayed if we changed our nationality from Dutch to Indonesian, but it was a matter of principle."

The Bruggemans left Indonesia, their home and paradise, in 1957 to move to the Netherlands—the country from which their people descended. They didn't see a future for their children in their home country. Many Dutch citizens including George's parents and other family members left the country. Not many Dutch nationals returned to the Netherlands because they had such a good life in Indonesia—plenty of work and food. But the Bruggemans gave up their family coconut plantation and fish farm for a life of the unknown because they were not willing to relinquish their Dutch heritage. "If I leave, I have to leave it all behind. So many friends wanted us to stay, even those working for the police department. When I told them all we were leaving, they were stunned. I'm Dutch. I cannot deny that," George said. The servants—mostly older than George—were crying and continued to ask why they had to go away knowing fully the reason why.

Albert and Emily Bruggeman were deeply affected by the communists' terror as well. Communists bombed their home because the military camp was close and was targeted. George remembers when his parents came to his house for shelter. His mother was pushing a baby stroller with her mother (George's grandmother) in it. Years before when Emily's mother found out that her youngest son had been killed in the war, she was never the same. George's grandmother never walked again from the grief and lived in a vegetative state until her death.

Even though the Netherlands was led by the Dutch Royal Family who sought resources in the 1600s in what would become Indonesia, war and greed dismantled the colony and its economy. The Netherlands had become one of the richest countries after the war because of all the wealth gathered from Indonesia, so the Bruggemans left for the Netherlands with one suitcase per person. They boarded a boat to Singapore with their four children and ultimately took an airplane to the Netherlands. Their tropical wardrobe left them cold and so did the attitude of the people of Holland. The entire family felt the disdain of nationalism: George's parents and the younger Bruggeman children felt the stigma of being transplanted, so they were still considered immigrants. Jans said, "It was like being Jew but marked a Dutch. [We would hear] 'Oh, they are Dutch!' They were so hateful."

(Bruggeman Family in 1959 before leaving Holland)

Fortunately, the family shared a house with two other families who gave them food and some clothing. But George and Jans found living in Holland to be a challenge, in part because George struggled to find a job and to advance his career. He applied for job after job after job. He was qualified, and most of the time overqualified based on his previous income, but no one would hire him. After months, he finally realized why. When asked why he could not get a job, he simply pointed to his forearm. The Bruggeman's were born in the Dutch East Indies and had darker complexions. In Holland, everybody was lighter skinned and looked down on the darker skinned people.

> "Some people look down on us. The kids in the neighborhood were fighting with our kids and calling them Chinese because of how they look different. We were foreigners to them," George said. "No matter who you marry, you are Dutch by blood. In America, you are American. If your parents are American but you are born in China, you are Chinese. If you are born somewhere, you are native to that country. But being Dutch goes by your forefather's blood. It doesn't matter where you're born or who you marry. That is why we are different compared to those in Holland."

The Bruggeman name finally helped George gain employment. He was hired because a previous captain in the army recognized the Bruggeman name on the application and immediately said he would give him a job. The captain who hired George acknowledged the racism that the family felt. He was trained and became a controller. George said, "I beat them all in smarts and became an inspector." Both George and Jans were relieved to have a source of income.

Still not equipped for the colder weather, Jans recalled how George rode a scooter to work with only a thin rain jacket as the snow blew in the sky. Jans remembered riding a bus 30 minutes to see her mother-in-law in the cold weather. "Sometimes the driver would come and sometimes not," she said. Even with employment and a new three-story home, the Bruggeman family could no longer withstand the mistreatment by others. Jans said none of it was worth being miserable. And after two years in Holland, George said, "The hell with it! I'm out of here." He did not see a future for their kids and decided to go to America.

While living in Rotterdam (just south of Amsterdam), Jans remembered a few memorable events. One was seeing Queen Wilhelmina in her golden coach parading down the street. The coach was used to carry her from the palace to the parliament building to deliver the speech from the throne. Jans also saw Queen Elizabeth during her time there. Another happy memory was the marriage of George's sister who married an officer from the Dutch army (who died young while serving in the Dutch colony of Suriname). And finally, the birth of their fifth child, while in Holland. With their sights set on a greater life in America, they named him Arlis—after their friend in Texas.

As the family prepared to leave Holland, a place that had become cold to them both literally and figuratively, George and Jans recognized the trials that lie ahead. Jans and the children spoke no English, and George only knew a little from high school plus the bits he had picked up in the prisoner of war camp. People told him it would be rough going to a country where he didn't know the language and where he had no job or home, but George assured everyone he would make it since he had already been through so much in his life and had the strength to endure it. Jans' mother and siblings lived with George and Jans until they left for Holland. Eventually her mother and brothers would immigrate to Holland too. But at the time, Jans' mother and siblings (sisters, Bea

(BAY-UH) and Taatge along with brothers, Nono and Pete) remained in the Netherlands, so the goodbye was not easy.

AMERICA

Sponsored to the States by Jans' cousin, George boarded his family of seven on a ship for the long journey across the ocean. During this time, the United States allowed only a certain number of immigrants from the Netherlands to enter each year, so the Bruggemans were grateful to be included in this number. To complicate the situation before leaving on the trip, Baby Arlis, born in 1959, was sick with an ear ache, so Jans begged a doctor to give her some medicine for the trip that would soothe his pain. Once off the ship, the family came into New York City and then boarded a train to Ohio.

While on the train, they met a man from Philadelphia who listened to their story. He played with the kids and asked where they would be living. Later, when they stepped off the train, a big box of toys—dolls for the girls and animals for the boys—arrived for the five children from this nice man. Jans corresponded with him and his wife throughout the years by writing letters. "That was the first person we met in America," Jans said.

In addition, a rental house had been arranged for them in Dayton. Parishioners of a local Catholic church paid the first month's rent. Also, furniture had been donated and the cupboards were stocked with groceries. They felt blessed to receive such a warm welcome. Jans said, "It felt like home all of a sudden because it was warm and green." Ohio's spring temperature was similar to that of the dry season in the mountains of Indonesia that she remembered so fondly.

But once again, it was difficult for George to secure a job with a wage comparable to the one in which he was accustomed. He was told he was overqualified when employers looked at his credentials. He begged them to allow him to clean the restrooms or sweep the floors. Then Jans' cousin, who was a piano player in a club across from Rike's department store in downtown Dayton, George finally got a job washing dishes in the Rike's cafeteria. "I had never washed a dish in my life because we had so many servants in the house," George said. He felt humiliated to wash dishes for a living after all of his previous responsibilities but was grateful for the chance to earn money. (George holding a carp)

"We had no money that first year, so we went to the butcher shop where they used stuff like beef lung and tripe for dog and cat food. I said, 'How much is that?' They said, 'Do you have animals?' and I said, 'No, but we want it.' And I got a pole and fished for carp in the river too," George said. "Nobody here [Dayton] ate carp, but we did."

In the end, he was offered the chance to begin working in the tailor shop moving clothes from downstairs to upstairs in the tailor's shop. "I was just to transport the clothes. I was happy because I was making more than $1 an hour at the time," George said. Jans was taking care of the kids, and George didn't want her to work. He continued to ask if there was more work he could do. They asked if he wanted to *learn* to tailor. He obliged and later used his newly acquired skills working in Kettering at a recently-opened men's shop. Combining his experience counting money as a kid and measuring for men's garments in the tailor shop, customers discerned his accuracy and precision. If George was not there to measure, the customer would often leave and come back later just to have *him* measure for them. Eventually, using all of his skills, George became a controller and furniture inspector for Rike's.

It was not long before George sponsored his parents to travel to the States. They lived with George and Jans for a time and then moved into the neighborhood. George's father, Albert, walked downtown each morning and spoke to every person he met on the street. But at lunchtime, he was never late for the soap opera, *As the World Turns* that helped him learn English. "Baller (the family nickname for Jans), I'm going to go," Albert said. "I'll be back at 12 o'clock." Jans recalled him running back at the last minute proclaiming how late he was and saying, "Turn it on! Turn it on!" She described how he pulled a chair right in front of the television to see that soap opera.

Before long, the sixth and final Bruggeman child was born. With his family complete and having lived a year and a half in Ohio, George and Jans sponsored family members to join them in the United States: his parents (with the help of a pastor); his sister, husband and child; his two brothers; a cousin; and his aunt who went to California and became a Mormons. His aunt then sponsored her parents and siblings who also settled in California. "At least 40 people came in this country through me. And all I had when I got off of the boat there in New York was $85," George said. He carried only one suitcase, while their furniture was shipped to Ohio by the Dutch government.

In 1970, George and Jans opened the *Frontier House* restaurant in what used to be the Forest Park shopping center. They served American food and were known for their brick-oven pizzas. Once a month, customers would line up to eat Jans' Indonesian egg rolls and other Indonesian foods. George was still working a full-time job, while Jans cooked at the restaurant. George would come home from his job, then work at the restaurant until it closed late at night to enable Jans to go home and care for the kids. She soon agreed that it was too much work for both of them.

> "I was at the restaurant every day. I help him. In the night, if he needs me, I went because always people are dancing and I would go. He is all alone. He called me. 'Meid

> (Dutch word for girl), come here.' In the winter, sometimes I ask myself. How could I dare? I was younger but had so many accidents bumping into things with the car."

Jans tells the story of coming to the restaurant around 5 o'clock one morning with George. She saw a man frying a ribeye steak! She spoke to the man: "What the hell is going on here?" She yelled for George who was already retrieving his revolver. The burglar ran, so George said, "Hon, grab him!" Jans jumped on his back, fell to the floor with him, pulled his long hair, and sat on it. The man who cleaned for them called the police. Jans said, "He told me to hold him until the police come, so I held him." George held the gun to the man's head, and the police pulled their gun on George thinking *he* was the intruder! Jans clarified that he was her husband. After the event, the burglar threw up in the police car, and both George and Jans laughed at the thought since he had stolen the food. Later, the customers joked they should all be careful of Jans: 'She will take you down!' After many successful years of managing the restaurant, but by the early 1980s, they decided to sell it because drugs were infiltrating the neighborhood.

When asked about his hobbies, George named fishing and hunting, and dancing, of course. But the one that might surprise most is to hear him mention soccer. In Dayton, many call him the grandfather of soccer. George inspired a man named Jerry Butcher to begin coaching soccer. Butcher owned a business and eventually coached soccer at the University of Dayton. He owned a pro team and ran an indoor soccer business. Dayton did not have any soccer teams when George arrived, and by 1962, George and his Dutch friends started a team: the Holland American Club. George played and coached soccer well into his 70s.

(George hunting after retirement)

Retirement did not slow down George's activities. In fact, he and his younger brother, Rudy, loved to swim and fish in Florida just like they had done in Celebes. They used nets to catch lobsters while snorkeling. "If the lobsters were not big enough, we had to throw them back. We were only allowed so many lobsters; authorities would fine you and take your boat," George said. He recalled one trip when he rose to the surface of the water with a snorkeling mask. He removed the mask to eat some crackers and struggled to bite the cracker. It didn't take him long to realize his upper dentures were missing! When removing his snorkel mask, he had pulled out the teeth and didn't realize it. George said, "Somewhere a lobster has a nice set of teeth!"

THE FAMILY (Bruggemans left to right: Linda, Ingrid, Edith, Jans, George, George Jr., Arlis, Dwight)

The Bruggemans are very proud of their children. George is grateful he came to America to give his kids a good life. He is proud that all have "made something of themselves." The daughters were all born first: Edith Constance was born in 1948 and became a hairdresser. The next year brought Ingrid Patricia who worked for a local hospital, and the next year Rosalinda Evaline who was a flight attendant. George Christian Jr. (who is called Georgie by the family) was the last to be born in Indonesia in 1953. He worked with George at the restaurant but was asked to come to work at a machine shop in Dayton. Edith was 12 when they boarded the ship to the United States and was a helpmate to Jans and the other children. Arlis Hendrick claimed he is the only true Dutchman since he was born six months before leaving Holland. He has worked in the restaurant business and is a restaurant manager. Dwight Douglas was born in 1966 and was named after George's two heroes: Dwight Eisenhower and Douglas Douglas McCarthy. Dwight worked as a manager at a machine shop for 30 years before pastoring a church.

    None of the children nor Jans spoke a word of English when the family left Holland, but George quickly taught them to say good morning. A pastor told Jans to learn English by watching television. "I listened to him and I learned," she said. The children swiftly learned English from other children in the neighborhood and at school. George and Jans saw the children grow and learn so much in the first ten years of living in Ohio. By working hard and being good parents, George and Jans called their family successful. He considered the family to be "well off," not necessarily in dollars but in happiness. That, he said, was their goal.

    George said he only wished his children could have grown up with an Indonesian experience, but the country was changing and it wasn't a good idea to remain there by the time his kids were growing up. Still, the kids learned a lot about the language and culture, even though they were miles from the islands of their origin. The couple spoke Dutch at home and with the kids. "We never lost our dialect after all these years," Jans said. The adult children understood Dutch but did not speak it fluently. George and Jans laughed at their kids' misuse of words and phrases, even today as their kids have grown into grandparents, Jans teases them when they speak. Meals eaten at home were mostly Indonesian, and all of the children know how to cook traditional dishes—including some of the in-laws! Indonesian foods are required at the large, annual Christmas party.

Most of the family in Holland and Indonesia have died; however, George's sister still lives in Holland and is desperate to come to the United States again, but for more than just a visit. She regrets not moving to the States earlier but is now too frail to travel. She plans to be cremated and buried in Dayton with her family—reunited after all these years. Jans had a girlfriend who longed to come as well but didn't have enough money to live in America.

Because George and Jans are skilled friend makers, they have entertained numerous friends and family in their home from abroad. One of their friends requested that his ashes be sent to George. "I told the kids and my wife: I want this urn in my coffin. Another friend who served as my brother and lived several years here also goes in my case [casket]."

The last time Jans visited Holland, right before her mother died, was the last she saw her siblings, and now they have all died. She laments the fact that she felt like she was separated from them for most of her life.

"Sometimes I think, why? Why did they leave me alone here? Everybody is gone. Why? I always take care of them, always," Jans said. I have two brothers, two sisters. My mom stayed in Indonesia with her sons and daughters. She didn't want to come to the States. She was old and blind. She was already sick the last time I saw her. She called my sister-in-law to get her bag. She had all of her gold stuff in that bag. She give me some jewelry: 'And this is for you and this is for all the daughters.'" Jans said, "The boys all got brand new blouses, like Hawaiian blouses. And she knows which one is which even though she cannot see. 'I am giving so you can remember me,' she said. It is the last time. It helps me to remember that suffering on this earth is nothing compared to Jesus' suffering. You must thank him and ask forgiveness.

Jans gave birth to her children in military hospitals. George was in the band playing when their fourth child and first son, Georgie, was born. George was desperate for a son. So when Jans gave birth to Georgie, she sent one of their friends to tell George he had a boy! He came immediately to see him and then returned to

(Jans at her daughter's wedding early 1970s) play with the band. (A father did not stay at the hospital or help their wives deliver babies like is done today.) Jans said, "It seemed I was pregnant every year! I was afraid every time that I'd be pregnant." Her mother-in-law was pregnant with her last child at the same time Jans was pregnant with her first. George's youngest brother Rudy was born two months before Edith. "Rudy is always with us," Jans said. Everywhere we go, he is there." Her second child was a 'blondine' and fat! People said she must be a kid from the milkman since her hair was so light.

ANCESTRY

George spoke fondly of his grandfather who started his life as a clerk and eventually rose to the position of governor. He described him as a man with great will power, and he was saddened that he never met him since he died before George was born. George's grandfather fought in the Aech War (the northern part of Sumatra, close to Singapore), a war fought over possession of some of the islands that could make Europeans rich. Indonesia housed gold, spices, diamonds, and other resources of interest. George described how big the ships were and how when sailing near each other, they resembled the Spanish Armada. His grandfather fought with bamboo spears on big sailboats. One time when his grandfather was fighting in a boat, he saw a boy who had fallen out and was trying to stay afloat in the war-torn water. Because he was an enemy, George's grandfather's comrades began beating the teenage boy with long oars.

"My grandfather said, 'Give him a life!' So he

rescued the boy and took him home," George told. "Maybe because of the hits on his head, the boy could not talk. My grandfather kept him alive, called him Sape (SOP-EH), and raised him as one of our servants."

This boy became a guardian to George. When his grandfather died, George's parents took care of Sape. He was trained to take and pick up George from school each day, and Sape became very protective of George throughout his life. His mind was never the same after the beating he endured in the water, so when George went to war, Sape did not fully understand why George had gone. George could not describe Sape's glee when he returned from war. It was George's pleasure to offer Sape cigarettes and see how happy he was. When George's parents left for the Netherlands, they entrusted Sape to George's uncle. It was only a couple years after George and Jans left for the Netherlands that Sape died a natural death.

Pride showed in George's body for all he had accomplished in this life, but that pride sat firmly next to shame and sadness. Territories in that day had their own kingdoms and languages, and in a southern province of Celebes where the Bugis lived, his grandfather married the Buginese princess. "Well, he didn't marry her," he said. "But he had three sons with the princess." A quiver rose in his voice as he wrestled with what he considered unethical behavior. Because of that position of power as governor, his grandfather never officially married the princess; nonetheless, the princess <u>was</u> George's grandmother. "I never have peace with that," George said. "If you fathered three kids, why is the position that you have more important than the kids that you brought in this world? I can't take that."

The name Bruggeman is very well known in Celebes, at least in the lower part of the country, because of the union between George's grandparents. The Bruggeman family was treated well and known widely. The grandfather was of Dutch descent and the princess was Indonesian. As the story goes, when the three sons were ready to go to school, they needed a last name in order to be accepted into the school. The grandfather's Dutch name was Brugeman spelled with one G. To ensure the children would have a name with a proper reputation since they were born of a Buginese woman and a Dutch man, the grandfather asked Carlo Bruggeman, a local bridge builder, if he could use the double G version of the name for his children. The man agreed, and the name has been spelled with two G's ever since. "We call him Uncle Carlo because he gave us our name," George said.

After all of the hardship the people of Indonesia endured, George never felt appreciated for serving in the service. The displacement and upending of families was a debt that could never be repaid. Records indicate that at least one million people died in Indonesia as a result of the Japanese occupation. Years later, the country of Indonesia paid the Dutch government so the government could pay a monetary settlement to all those who lost their homes and possessions and family. This fact was never made public though, and 70 years later, the government agreed to pay it to the people. The government kept the money until this time to use for the country and most of those who were owed were already dead. Finally after all those years, the Bruggeman's were paid $28,000.

FOR THE FUTURE GENERATIONS

George was adamant about the problems of this world

today. He said it is most important to forget about the differences between races. In a world without love, George fears for the future generations.

> "I don't care what color you are, I love you. If I love you, then I know I will get love back. It's doesn't matter your skin. You cannot hate," George said. "If you have love for each other, then you will become a completely different person. It does not matter if you believe in Mohammed or Christ or Buddha. One calls it Allah, we call it God. He's our creator—He's all the same thing. You wake up in the morning and see these birds and flowers. Who made those? Not one people but the Almighty God made that. There is one thing I always try to get my kids and grandkids to remember: don't ever fear. If you believe in the Almighty God, then there should not be fear. Because He will decide what is going to happen with you. You just have to be happy with it."

George believed in accepting a thank you graciously and in being humble because it is all that brings peace in life. After those years in war, he struggled to reconcile war. He asked, "Why would a God of love allow it?" But George believed a reason existed for all things, including a time to die.

> "If my God says, you know what George, you have served your purpose. It's your time to go, then I will go with a smile. I know I will be going back to my Creator. He created us, and He has the power and the love to handle what He needs to handle for us. I am not afraid of death,"

George said. "You cannot live in fear. If you are afraid of death, you don't believe. That is what I always try to make people understand. Before someone dies, if they ask the Lord for forgiveness, they will be happy. They will be back to him. They will have no sorrows anymore, no pain or anything. I want to be remembered as a person who is happy and humble and loving. That is the way I will be remembered."

Jans believed similarly. She was never able to finish high school and would like to have had an education. She knew that her grandchildren's generation would never experience hunger the way she and her family did and so many others in history.

"All the kids today waste food. Throw it out! I hate that because it's still good! We have to be grateful to God for all we have and thank Him," she said. "We live and we all have difficulties, but we have to be thankful. I really thank Him for having him [George] with me still. I have to be grateful."

George fully believed life was not about money or power. He said it did not matter if a person lived in poverty or in the wilderness. Those people have feelings just like those who have money and power. He believed in taking care of his possessions and hoped young people might choose to learn from old things and not just toss them aside. "Stuff from 300 years ago should still exist and be respected." George expressed regret for not spending more time with his elders.

> "My dad has teach me an awful lot of things. I love him very much, but I didn't give him really the time and show him the love I have for him. My oldest boy does," George said. "Every night, he calls us—every night. Feeling the love from my son like that makes me think 'Why didn't I ever have the time for my dad? I was always working, doing this and that. Why didn't I ever show my love to my dad that way?'"

He believed in knowing where your ancestors came from, not just what continent they lived on but really knowing where they were born and who they were as a family.

WITH AN END, A BEGINNING

As the recorder of these stories, I cannot be unaffected by the love that oozes from these two people. They have sustained such hardship and mistreatment by many people but remained steadfast to the belief in the goodness of humankind. They have lived fully (and are not yet finished) a life that God ordained just for them. A verse from the book of Hebrews fittingly depicts the perseverance and longevity of this couple:

> "Therefore, since we are surrounded by such a great cloud of witnesses, let us throw off everything that hinders and the sin that so easily entangles. And let us run with perseverance the race marked out for us." Hebrews 12: 1

Whether someone has known George and Jans for a lifetime or only a few minutes, I am certain each person who has come into contact with them has felt their compassion for their fellow human.

(George's 95th birthday party)

Before George needed a walker, he could be found dancing with the ladies at a family party. The kids all told him to take it easy and have a seat, fearing he might fall. But he assured them he would not and the music seemed to take over his body.

On one visit I made to the hospital, George was a bit sad about not being home. I turned my phone to the dance music he loves, and he could not help but move to the rhythm. When visiting the house, the door was almost always unlocked and upon knocking, a voice called out, "Come in!" Jans generally peeked out from the kitchen doorway to say hello, and the smell of something yummy on the stove greeted the visitor. I always knew going to see them meant I would be served a drink and probably a bowl of Indonesian food, whether I was hungry or not.

At the time of these interviews, George and Jans were struggling with having to be more and more dependent on others. The issue of independence—and the lack of it seems to have been a yarn in the life of this couple. George was tossed into war and grew into independence quickly by killing and following orders to survive. The Bruggeman children are now escorting George in the car rather than letting him drive it himself. In her childhood, Jans cared for her siblings and ran errands for her mother as her father was away and dying in the war. And now the Bruggeman children are trying to keep her from using the heavy pots and pans in her own kitchen. Their sense of independence is strong, like most folks of their generation. George growls and raises his voice when others want to push him in a wheelchair, and Jans talks back with sarcasm like a teenager to her children: "Helloooo!" They are averse to saying goodbye to living alone and not climbing the stairs as they have done for over 70 years together.

And now as the final sentences of this book are formed, George and Jans have left the comfort of their home and are clinging to the moments they have together. And after using his body to its fullest extent, a good day for George is a shower, a well-made bed, a juicy hamburger, and having the love of his life in his sight. The battle he fights now is keeping hope in his mind and in his heart—filling the end of life with courage and confidence. Jans is motivated to dress each morning—complete with makeup and jewelry—just to venture across the facility's campus to check on the other half of her heart. She loves a good story and laughs whole heartedly whenever she can. She enjoys beautiful keepsakes and her own cooking, but her finest treasure is the love she shares with George. I and the countless others who have been given the opportunity to know George and Jans have experienced an outpouring of the most genuine love and extraordinary friendship.

> "Hope deferred makes
> the heart sick,
> but a longing fulfilled is
> a tree of life"
> Proverbs 13:12

ABOUT THE AUTHOR

Heidi Arnold is a college professor who enjoys writing poetry and non-fiction. She writes this sweet and bitter story out of her love for people with adorable wrinkles, rich tales, and a foot close to Heaven. She's published several poems and stories and most recently was the second place winner of the Antioch Writers' Workshop Bill Baker Scholarship for non-fiction.

Made in the USA
Middletown, DE
31 January 2019